ZENSHO W. KOPP

The ascent
of the inner
Light

Our lives are as fleeting and impermanent as a dew drop, hanging from the tip of a blade of grass.

The entire universe is subject to a constant process of change and is thus impermanent. However, your true essence is immutability. It is eternal being and thus immortal.

Meditation opens a path for us to the unending, inner space that reveals itself to us in its timeless eternity.

Meditation allows the mind to mature towards a state of constant awareness of the presence of the all-fulfilling wholeness of divine reality that encompasses us. When we experience this, the duality of Samsara and Nirvana dissolves away.

Your true essence is the reality of pure being that manifests itself when thinking ceases.

It is the gleaming, eternal, self-existing original essence of divine being, which lies at the base of all the three states: being awake, dreaming and deep sleep.

In each person, this divine light radiates as the true self.

The aim of all sublime mysticism is that by realising spiritual clarity, you see through the empty nature of all phenomena and awaken to the reality of the One Mind, which is beyond space and time.

See things as they really are and recognise that everything is a revelation of the reality of the One Mind.

True meditation is a consciousness state in which you are the neutral witness. As the silent observer behind all experiences you are just witness to what takes place.

Your thoughts, drifting over the self-mind, are like passing clouds that appear and disappear. They are illusory and have no essence of their own.

By realising a consciousness within us that is completely undivided and dwells on nothing, we achieve a clear perception of our true being.

Reconnecting with this, our true essence, as our innermost core being and becoming one with it is the true goal of our human existence.

The One Mind, existing of itself, is the light of your original buddha-nature and the innermost essence of all things.

Your whole world-experience is merely a projection of your discriminating consciousness. Behind it, beyond birth and death, your true essence radiates with undiminished clarity.

Driven by the force of habit of your conditioned consciousness, you wander lost, in the cycle of birth and death.

Whatever you may achieve in life, it can give you no ultimate, lasting satisfaction. You will only experience this when you have achieved your true essence.

Dying into the dark abyss of divine nothingness is the great awakening to the reality of our true essence.

The secret of immortality is unity with God.

Through this unity, the awakened one breaks through the cyclic force of birth and death and experiences themselves as eternal, immortal reality; the radiating light of the One Mind.

Zen meditation is about immersing yourself in the experience of your own essence. Here you perceive all-pervading reality, free of all images.

In the light of this pure perception, everything dissolves that does not belong to what you are and your true, immortal self reveals itself.

Your mind becomes silent and clear when you allow it to abide naturally in the open vastness of the absolute present moment of Here and Now.

View your thoughts with a consciousness that does not think. When all is silent within you and you constantly view your own mind, you are on the true path to liberation.

A true person of Zen is constantly the master of his own self and does not become a slave to human sentiment.

You can only awaken when you have peace within you. Thus, realise the consciousness of a detached observer behind all experiences so that, in inner tranquillity, you achieve an unswervingly cheerful and relaxed reflection of the mind.

When your mind is pure and empty, all things are pure and empty.

In reality, there are no problems but just self-perpetuating, discriminating thoughts. However, the intellect cannot grasp this since it is only made up of thoughts itself.

The more the thinking lessens, the more the cheerfulness and clarity of the mind appear of their own accord since they are the natural state of your true being.

I am Buddha and you are Buddha. There is no other Buddha. We are Buddha since nothing else exists other than Buddha, the true self.

When you recognise that your own mind as your true essence is Buddha, the mystery of Zen reveals itself to you.

Finding God means recognising Him and being absolutely one with Him. However, this is no perception performed by the senses or any form of intellectual insight but rather a direct, pure spiritual experience.

A God-loving person in mystical immersion who perceives God in His naked reality is so One with Him that he experiences himself as God.

In unmoved seclusion of the mind you are in the fullness of being and your mind is empty and clear.

Since your true self is as pure and as radiating as the sun, you need only take care that your mind becomes completely relaxed and vast and clear, just like the heavens, so that the realisation of your true being shines forth.

Through constant awareness of the present moment we can break through the power of all deceptive thoughts and concepts and achieve spiritual clarity.

In the moment-consciousness of Now you enter into the spacelessness and timelessness of pure being and recognise that the present moment is eternal.

You do not need to seek the Kingdom of God for it is constantly present within you as your immortal, true self.

Here and Now, transcending the dualistic perception of subject and object, your true self reveals itself as the eternal, original source of everything.

Your mind becomes clear when you see through the illusory nature of all phenomena.

Everything you perceive is just phenomena within your own mind and thus the mind itself. Nothing comes from beyond the mind. When you recognise your true self, everything you see, wherever you look, is reality.

When you realise your true essence, you are inwardly empty and in unison with external things.

Therefore, make your mind pure and clear like a mirror, which reflects everything without identification and attachment, and you will be beyond all worldly entanglement.

In order to achieve your true essence, the scattered, restless mind must become silent and clear.

When you are inwardly silent and clear, so that external things have no influence over you, you reach the profound experience of intentionless awareness without any effort on your part.

When this profound, clear self-awareness constantly abides within you will have great peace everywhere and at all times.

You can only liberate yourself from the dualism of discriminating thinking through the clarity of mind accomplished in Zen meditation.

Through this power of non-thinking, the mind shines like the clear sky in the boundless expanse of the void and nothing can darken it anymore.

One moment of being touched by divine love in inner mystical contemplation has more value than the knowledge of all the holy scriptures and philosophies.

Transform your urge for intellectual understanding into a silent awareness of your fundamental nature.

Turn your mind inwards and immerse yourself in pure bliss.

In the immutable nature of the mind, where phenomena, consciousness and void are a perfect, self-existing entity, there is no distinction between Samara and Nirvana.

This pure, original dimension of your mind is the unchanging nature of the great void, which lies beyond existence and non-existence.

When your senses do not deceive you, you will see that all things are the light of the mind. With great clarity and effortless, open awareness you transcend the ordinary world.

When you have become one with the fundamental essence, you will experience that the true mind is an unmoving, boundless void and that your true being is free from birth and death.

The true self-mind is the empty, radiating nature of being.

This eternally radiating light of the One Mind is our intrinsic, true self. It is completely detached from the illusions of a space-time existence and all its multitudinous forms in which it appears to us.

Meditation means consciously sinking into the inner ground. Here, you become aware of your immortal true essence and you lose all fear of death.

However, it is only possible to awaken from the dream of birth and death through the blessing of divine grace.

Liberation from your autonomous, compulsive thinking can only take place through an absolute presence of the mind in the present moment.

Through this power of inner awareness you rise above the illusion of space and time and all attachments.

When you have liberated yourself from your discriminating thinking and have thus grasped the original essence of your own mind, you eradicate all ignorance.

In the silence of mystical immersion, your birthless and deathless true self reveals itself.

You are always in eternity, even when you are not aware of it. It is only your thinking that creates the notion of time.

Look into your innermost self, for the truth you are seeking is closer to you than you are to yourself.

The entire world of phenomena is just a projection in the consciousness. It only has a relative existence, just like that of a mirage.

It is not a question of now rejecting the world but of altering our outlook on things and thus dissolve all attachments to them.

The way of inwardly letting go of everything that is not God leads us directly to the divine light.

This experience of divine light is the revelation of divine love and takes place solely through grace.

The more a person is prepared to give themselves to the Absolute, the more they will receive grace as the action of the divine Being.

When you die into the abyss of the divine void, your original countenance before your birth reveals itself.

Death can catch us unexpectedly, whether we are prepared for it or not. Therefore, die before you die so that your inner eye opens before your external eye for ever closes.

The external world of phenomena is a game of the mind. If you take it to be real, you will be deceived by the images in your own mind.

Everything is but a mere illusory spectacle. Mind is the sole reality and beyond Mind, nothing exists whatsoever.

Zen always points with absolute directness to the original state of our true essence – immediately and directly.

In the depths of the heart there is no division between you and God. Here, you are united with God. The experience of this unity, which transforms your whole being, is the revelation of what you have always been, currently are and will always be.

If you wish to be blessed with grace as the working of divine love, there is no other way than for you to withdraw yourself in your actions and your wanting, so that divine love can act within you.

Become an empty vessel so that you become filled with the fullness of divine being.

Make your mind completely free from before and after, without any limitations and attach yourself to nothing.

Act and abide in non-action – this is correct action in unison with the Tao.

When you abide in the midst of things, without them influencing you, you are in harmonic unison with heaven and earth.

The Zen way requires great determination and strength of mind, plus an uninterrupted intensity of concentration of true awareness.

It requires you to use great determination to make your mind completely clear of all hindrances, so that all actions and endeavours originate from the primal source.

When, in your mystical immersion, you reach the boundary of life and death, you enter into absolute silence and your mind expands into boundlessness.

This all-transforming experience of our true, original nature, beyond birth and death is the great awakening from the dream of a three-dimensional world in space and time.

Since everything is fleeting and impermanent, put your whole effort into achieving your unfading, eternal self.

The true self radiates in its own light. Its power is endless and beyond the perception of the senses. It is the source of all experience and whoever perceives it is free from birth and death.

At the heart of our innermost being, the divine light shines. Thus, the highest experience in life is the awakening to this, our true self.

In inner silence your mind is illuminated by divine light and embraced by a mysterious plenitude of love.

True immersion means abiding in silent observation of your own, true self.

This perception of the eternal essential-ground takes place when you tune in to the inexhaustible, divine depths. It is when you become aware of the Eternal within you.

By immersing yourself in the depths of your own essence, you experience the divine presence within you and all things.

Only within you can the mystery of all mysteries reveal itself.

True self-perception is true perception of God.

The highest realisation of the mind lies in its pure perception of itself as eternal, highest reality and in the absolute unification with it as perfect love.

Pure love constantly seeks to overcome all opposites for it strives for consummate love.

The power of divine love does not allow your heart to come to rest until it has completely immersed itself in God.

When you have overcome the darkness of ignorance through the purity of your true essence, you finally cut through your attachment to birth and death.

Through constant, dedicated immersion in your inner ground, you achieve an all-transcending realisation of eternal reality, which you experience in the depths of your consciousness as blissful Being.

The divine light shines forth in these inner-most depths and breaks through the darkness.

Only within yourself can you find silence and true peace, since there you are constantly united with divine love.

The source of your consciousness is form-less and invisible. There is no way to describe it or reflect on it. It can only be experienced directly.

Beyond all intellectual understanding, you plunge into the transcendental experience of divine glory.

In the silence of inner awareness, you enter into the Eternal.

If your mind is to become open and clear, you must firstly cast off all dualistic thinking and turn the light of the mind around so that it shines on itself.

When the confusion and restlessness in the mind cease, silent clarity arises. In this silence, transcendent wisdom appears of its own accord.

If you genuinely wish to awaken to your true essence, you must have boundless trust in divine reality.

Only by completely letting go and dying into the divine ground will the light appear that we all seek. Impenetrable to the senses and the intellect, it is the radiating splendour of our true self.

Wisdom and love belong inseparably together, for without love there cannot be any wisdom, and without wisdom there is also no true love.

By realising the essential equality of all beings you abide in all-encompassing love and embrace all beings in your heart.

The greater your trust in divine reality, the greater your devotion.

What really matters at the moment of death is boundless trust in divine reality. It is the certainty that instead of falling into nothingness, we will die into the unending splendour of divine being.

When your mind is empty and clear and dwells in effortless awareness, you achieve all-embracing consciousness.

In order to enter the transcendental experience of enlightenment, you need determination above all. Your mind must be clear and unwavering if the cycle of birth and death is to find an end.

True equanimity means that you abide in steadfastness of the mind in all of life's situations.

Wherever you are and whatever you are doing, turn inwards and abide in the spiritual clarity of your true self.

Train yourself to constantly retain this state of pure awareness, just as it is.

The pure, clear self-awareness of the mind is a boundless, open vastness, in which all phenomena dissolve in a natural way, without leaving any lasting impression behind.

However, those who cling to things, without recognising that they are just mind, attach themselves and do not recognise the true, empty nature of the mind.

Absolute devotion to the divine means turning inwards and forgetting yourself and all things. When you devotion is great enough, you will be devoured by divine grace.

When the divine light of perception shines in your heart, it will raise you into eternal bliss.

Your true essence is timeless consciousness, which outshines all duality.

The consciousness of the intellect is misled by a multitude of sense objects. The false conclusion is in seeing the inseparable One as something separate.

However, in pure awareness of mind, you rest in the original ground state of equality, in which sense objects and consciousness are experienced as one.

In your innermost essence you are divine reality. This reality is the fundamental, eternal essence, the origin of all phenomena in the universe.

This true, divine self is the divine light inherent within you, through which you live, you are aware and which enables you to perceive the world.

Impressum

First edition 2023

Original title "**Der Aufgang des inneren Lichtes**"
published by Spirit Rainbow Verlag, Aachen, Germany 2021

Image credits: shutterstock von Vladimir Kim
www.shutterstock.com/de/g/vladimirkim3722

Original idea and design: Verena Kopp
Image editing: Reinhard Zanella
Translation: John Kitching
Typesetting/ Cover design: Reinhard Zanella
Back cover photo: Axel Jung

© 2023, Zensho W.Kopp

Production and publishing:

BoD - Books on Demand, Norderstedt

ISBN: 9783757825102

Zensho W. Kopp, born 1938, is one of the most significant spiritual masters of our present times and teaches a contemporary path to spiritual realisation. The internationally renowned author of numerous Zen books and audio books instructs a large community of students and directs the Zen Center Tao Chan in Wiesbaden, Germany.

Tao Chan Zentrum e.V., Non-profit society, Wiesbaden.
More info at: **www.tao-chan.org**

Twice a month, the Zen Center Tao Chan organises an Zen-evening with a talk by Zen Master Zensho W. Kopp, where guests are welcome to attend. There is also the possibility for asking Zen Master Zensho questions.

Register here for the online evening:
www.tao-chan.org/events/events-zen-night.html

Zen Center Tao Chan
www.youtube.com/@zencentertaochan

Subscribe here for free short talks by Zen Master Zensho W. Kopp:
www.youtube.com/@zencentertaochan/shorts

Facebook site for the Zen Center Tao Chan
www.facebook.com/zencentertaochan

Books and audiobooks by Zensho W. Kopp

also available as **eBook** in ePUB and Kindle format

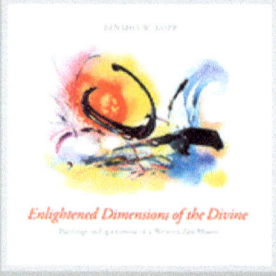

Modern ZEN-ART, Watercolours and sayings of a Western Zen Master.
124 pages, 23,50 €

Enlightened Dimensions of the Divine, Paintings and quotations of a Western Zen Master
140 pages, 10,50 €

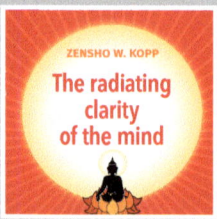

The Flame of Awareness
124 pages

Living in inner fullness
116 pages, 9,80 €

The power of inner quietude
104 pages, 9,80 €

The radiating clarity of the mind
136 pages

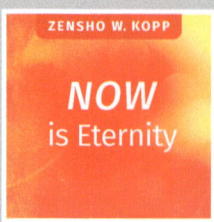

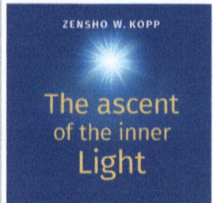

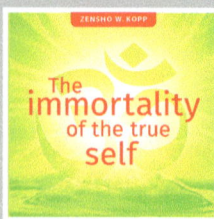

Now is Eternity
114 pages, 9,80 €

The ascent of the inner Light
114 pages

The immortality of the true self
104 pages

The mystery of true self-perception
124 pages

Books and audiobooks by Zensho W. Kopp

also available as **eBook** in ePUB and Kindle format

The ZEN Ox-herding Pictures
The path to Enlightment
212 pages, 9,95 €

True Life Through Zen
Spiritual self-realisation in daily life
140 pages, 11,50 €

Awakening to Your True Self
The Zen way of all-embracing mysticism
140 pages, 11,99 €

Lao-tse Tao Te King
The book of Tao and spiritual force
120 pages, 7,95 €

All publications by Zensho can be found and purchased here:
www.tao-chan.org/zen-master-zensho/books.html

Books and audiobooks by Zensho W. Kopp

also available as **eBook** in ePUB and Kindle format

**The Direct Zen-Way
to Liberation**
212 pages, 9,95 €

ZEN in daily life
187 pages

**Words of the
Awakened Mind**
140 pages, 9,95 €

The Freedom of ZEN
216 pages